God's Little Book of Peace

by David Marshall

Dedicated to Angela O'Brien

All texts are taken from the New International
Version unless otherwise stated

Amp – The Amplified Bible, Zondervan, 1965.
LB – Living Bible, Tyndale House 1971.
MGE – The Message: the Bible in Contemporary English.
Eugene H. Peterson. NavPress, 2002.
NKJV – New King James Version.
NLT – New Living Translation, Tyndale House Publishers, 1996.
Phillips – The New Testament in Modern English
by J. B. Phillips, Collins, 1972.
REB – Revised English Bible, Oxford and Cambridge, 1989.

Copyright © 2003
First published 2003
Reprinted 2009
All rights reserved. No part of this publication
may be reproduced in any form without prior
permission from the publisher.

British Library Cataloguing in Publication Data.
A catalogue record for this book is available
from the British Library.

ISBN 1-903921-12-0

Published by
Autumn House
Alma Park, Grantham, England.
Printed in Thailand

The Peace of Jesus

Over the broken pieces of our lives is the echo of Jesus offering his peace. ' "I am leaving you with a gift – peace of mind and heart," ' he said. ' "And the peace I give isn't like the peace the world gives. So don't be troubled or afraid." ' (John 14:27, NLT.)

The group of followers to whom Jesus originally spoke those words were oppressed by fears and forebodings. Some of their fears were focused on specific things; others were less specific, but nonetheless real for that. Their forebodings arose from their insecurities and lack of trust. They were, in a sense, then, a microcosm of the Christian church down through the ages; and, therefore, as individuals, random sample Christians.

The peace on offer to them and to us was and is not just the escape route from trouble, sorrow, suffering, guilt and danger. Nor is it just a profound sense of inner calm, though that is a part of it. It is more positive than tranquillity. *Shalom*-peace makes for our highest good. It is as much at home in the storm as in the calm that comes after. It is a supernatural gift that is more likely to be offered to those who face crisis than to those becalmed. And it was offered not just in the upper room but throughout scripture. This book collects together the words in which it was offered.

David Marshall

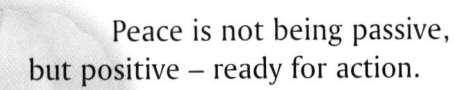

Peace is not being passive,
but positive – ready for action.

'Stand firm . . . with your feet fitted with the
readiness that comes from the gospel of peace.'
Ephesians 6:14, 15.

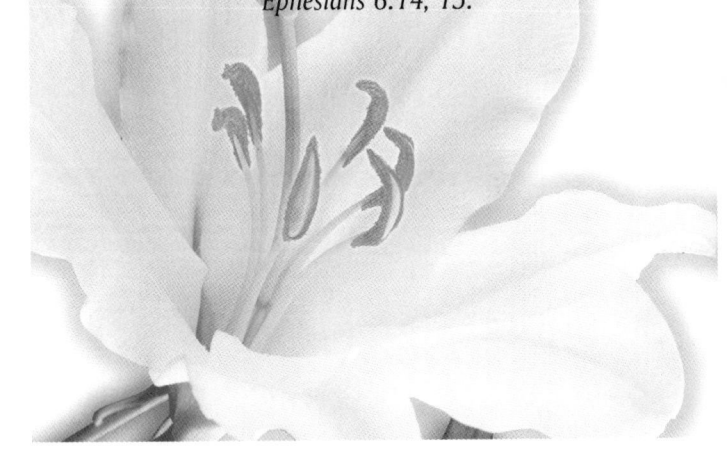

The foundation of peace is God and
the secret of peace is trust.

'The Lord bless you and keep you; . . . the Lord
turn his face towards you and give you peace.'
Numbers 6:24, 26.

Stand tall in the wide open spaces of God's grace – and grasp pardon and peace together.

'Since we have been made right in God's sight by faith, we have peace with God because of what Jesus Christ our Lord has done for us.'
Romans 5:1, NLT.

When Christ was born the angels sang of peace. When he was crucified he made peace possible for every believer.

'He will be called Wonderful Counsellor, Mighty God, Everlasting Father, Prince of Peace.'
Isaiah 9:6.

God is faithful. Serve him faithfully and he will provide for all your needs.

'You will keep in perfect peace him whose mind is steadfast, because he trusts in you.'
Isaiah 26:3.

If you are trusting in your own righteousness,
Christ died in vain.
The route to peace is through the
acceptance of his righteousness and pardon.

'Peacemakers who sow in peace raise
a harvest of righteousness.'
James 3:18.

The gift of peace is for sharing.

'Live in peace with each other.'
1 Thessalonians 5:13.

No one can live at peace with others,
let alone peace with himself,
unless first he has peace with God.

'Let the peace of Christ keep you in tune with
each other, in step with each other.'
Colossians 3:15, MGE.

Our hearts will be restless until we find rest in God. His rest, his peace, is good for all circumstances.

'The peace of God, which surpasses human understanding, will keep constant guard over your hearts and minds as they rest in Christ Jesus.'
Philippians 4:7, Phillips.

Peace does not come from treaties negotiated by politicians, but is a gift that comes as a product of citizenship of God's kingdom.

'The kingdom of God is . . . righteousness, peace and joy.'
Romans 14:17.

Jesus makes God's promises shine like the stars.
The darker the night, the brighter
he makes them shine.

'Jesus Christ, the Son of God . . . was himself no
doubtful quantity, he is the divine "Yes". Every
promise of God finds its affirmative in him.'
2 Corinthians 1:19-21, Phillips.

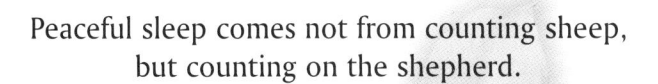

Peaceful sleep comes not from counting sheep, but counting on the shepherd.

'I will lie down and sleep in peace, for you alone, O Lord, make me dwell in safety.'
Psalm 4:8.

God gives peace and strength with the same hand. When God is our strength our peace is real. When our strength is our own, it is not; for our own strength is but weakness.

'The Lord gives strength to his people;
the Lord blesses his people with peace.'
Psalm 29:11.

God does not comfort us to make us
comfortable, but to make us comforters.
In the same way he gives us peace
to make us peacemakers.

'God . . . is our Father and the source of all
mercy and comfort. For he gives us comfort in
all our trials so that we in turn may be able to
give the same sort of strong sympathy to others
in their troubles that we receive from God.'
2 Corinthians 1:3-5, Phillips.

The only healers God uses are those who have been wounded first. Christ was wounded that we might be healed; our wounds enable us to be his healers in the world.

'The more we share in Christ's immeasurable suffering the more we are able to give of his encouragement.'
2 Corinthians 1:5, Phillips.

Peace comes to us in the desperate times only
when we have shifted our entire burden
on to God's broad shoulders.

'At that time we were completely overwhelmed,
the burden was more than we could bear, in
fact we told ourselves that this was the end.
Yet we believe now that we had this sense
of impending disaster so that we might learn
to trust, not in ourselves, but in God.'
2 Corinthians 1:8, 9, Phillips.

Our future is safe in God's hands,
as is our present and our past.

'We put our full trust in him and he
will keep us safe in the future.'
2 Corinthians 1:10, Phillips.

God loves us *in* our sin, and *through* our sin, and goes on loving us, looking for a response. Peace is given in exchange for that response.

'Turn your back on sin; do something good. Embrace peace – don't let it get away!'
Psalm 34:14, MGE.

Go-getters may get more than their fair share of the action; but the meek will inherit the Earth.

'The meek will inherit the land
and enjoy great peace.'
Psalm 37:11.

The future – long-term – belongs to the peacemakers. That is true even when the bullies appear to control the present.

'There is a future for the man of peace. . . .'
Psalm 37:37.

The man who says 'I'm no fool' usually has his
suspicions. . . . Peace road begins at the
point where folly is abandoned.

'I will listen to what God the Lord will say;
he promises peace to his people . . .
but let them not return to folly.'
Psalm 85:8.

Righteousness is a Godward relationship of trust and dependence. Peace is the gift God gives as a consequence of that relationship.

'Love and faithfulness meet together; righteousness and peace kiss each other.'
Psalm 85:10.

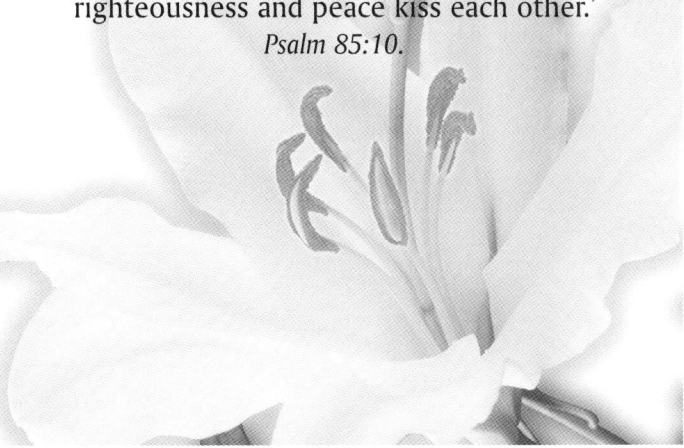

Peace is not a matter of choice, it is a matter of receiving. It is like a river that flows from the foot of an invisible throne, and flows by the channel of obedience.

'Great peace have they who love your law, and nothing can make them stumble.'
Psalm 119:165.

Don't be a bully! Especially not a spiritual bully!
If you want God to accept you,
it's a good start to accept others.

'Don't walk around with a chip on your
shoulder, always spoiling for a fight. . . .
"Why not?" you say. Because God
can't stand twisted souls.'
Proverbs 3:29, 30, MGE.

God has the map, knows the way, and has seen the weather forecast. So just drive!

'Trust God from the bottom of your heart; don't try to figure out everything on your own. Listen for God's voice in everything you do, everywhere you go; he's the one who will keep you on track.'
Proverbs 3:5, 6, MGE.

All barriers between man and man – broken down, dissolved, resolved in Jesus Christ. That is the formula for peace on Earth.

'In Christ Jesus you who once were far away have been brought near. . . . For he himself is our peace, who has made the two one and has destroyed the barrier, the dividing wall of hostility.'
Ephesians 2:13, 14.

An apple tree cannot help
producing apples. . . .

'The acts of the sinful nature are . . . hatred,
discord, jealousy, fits of rage, selfish
ambition. . . . But the fruit of the
Spirit is love, joy, peace. . . .'
Galatians 5:19, 20, 22.

Hold on!
Hold fast!
Hold out!

Jesus said 'You may find your peace in me. You will find trouble in the world – but, never lose heart, I have conquered the world!'
John 16:33, Phillips.

Do you get the message?

The risen Christ said, ' "Peace be with you!" '
John 20:19.
'Again Jesus said, "Peace be with you!" '
John 20:21.
'A week later . . . Jesus came and stood among them and said, "Peace be with you!" '
John 20:26.

The way of life is the way of peace.

'The mind of sinful man is death, but the mind controlled by the Spirit is life and peace.'
Romans 8:6.

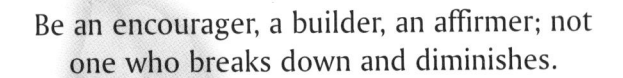

Be an encourager, a builder, an affirmer; not one who breaks down and diminishes.

'Let's agree to use all our energy in getting along with each other. Help others with encouraging words; don't drag them down by finding fault.'
Romans 14:19, MGE.

Messiah, King, Peacemaker.

' "But you, Bethlehem, . . . out of you will come
for me one who will be ruler over Israel,
whose origins are from of old. . . .
He will stand and shepherd his flock. . . .
And he will be their peace." '
Micah 5:2-5.

The way of peace is the way of freedom.

'Wherever the Spirit of the Lord is,
men's souls are set free.'
2 Corinthians 3:17, Phillips.

God cares, guides, protects and shields.

'Then the Lord will create over all of Mount Zion. . . . a shelter and shade from the heat of the day, and a refuge and hiding-place from the storm and rain.'
Isaiah 4:5, 6.

Storms make roots run deeper.

'Blessed is the man who trusts in the Lord, . . .
He will be like a tree planted by the water
that sends out its roots by the stream.'
Jeremiah 17:7, 8.

Just as a kite rises on the thermals, even the worst of troubles can give us strength.

'O Lord, you are my God; . . . You have been a refuge for the poor, a refuge for the needy in his distress, a shelter from the storm and a shade from the heat.'
Isaiah 25:1, 4.

Peace is the 'scent' of Christ discernable on his followers.

'Thanks be to God who leads us . . . on Christ's triumphant way and makes our knowledge of him spread . . . like a lovely perfume! We Christians have the unmistakable "scent" of Christ. . . .'
2 Corinthians 2:14, 15, Phillips.

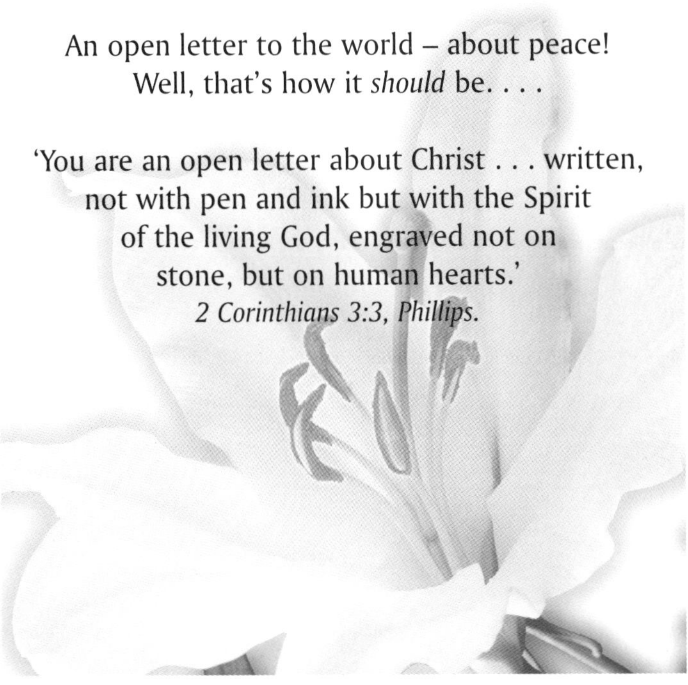

An open letter to the world – about peace!
Well, that's how it *should* be. . . .

'You are an open letter about Christ . . . written,
not with pen and ink but with the Spirit
of the living God, engraved not on
stone, but on human hearts.'
2 Corinthians 3:3, Phillips.

Peace – in the face of pressure, frustration, puzzlement and persecution: the peace of the presence of Christ.

'We are hard pressed on all sides, but we are never frustrated; we are puzzled, but never in despair. We are persecuted, but are never deserted: we may be knocked down but we are never knocked out!'

2 Corinthians 4:8, 9, Phillips.

God's sons and daughters make peace
from force of habit and because,
for them, it is natural.

'Blessed are the peacemakers; they
shall be called God's children.'
Matthew 5:9, REB.

If we pray for peace the very act immerses us in the spirit of peace – and the prayer is half way to being answered.

'Now may the Lord of peace himself give you peace at all times and in every way.'
2 Thessalonians 3:16.

Peace will have the last word!

'The wolf will live with the lamb, the leopard will lie down with the goat, the calf and the lion and the yearling together; and a little child will lead them.'
Isaiah 11:6.

Peace rules the day when Christ rules the heart.

'Grace and peace to you from him who is, and who was, and who is to come, . . . and from Jesus Christ, who is . . . the firstborn from the dead, and the ruler of the kings of the earth.'
Revelation 1:4, 5.

Peace, like rest, is something that cannot be made. It has to be entered into.

'There remains, then, a Sabbath-rest for the people of God; for anyone who enters God's rest also rests from his own work, just as God did from his.'
Hebrews 4:9, 10.

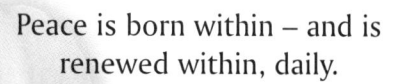

Peace is born within – and is
renewed within, daily.

'The outward man does indeed suffer wear
and tear, but every day the inward man
receives fresh strength.'
2 Corinthians 4:16, Phillips.

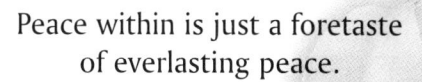

Peace within is just a foretaste
of everlasting peace.

'These hard times are small potatoes compared
to the coming good times, the lavish
celebration prepared for us. There's
far more here than meets the eye.'
2 Corinthians 4:17, MGE.

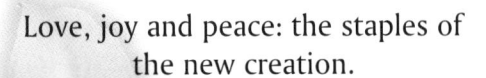

Love, joy and peace: the staples of
the new creation.

'If anyone is in Christ, he is a new creation;
the old has gone, the new has come!'
2 Corinthians 5:17.

If the Christian church is seen as a peaceful and loving community, the world will repent of its evil.

'We are . . . Christ's ambassadors, as though God were making his appeal through us. We implore you on Christ's behalf: Be reconciled to God.'
2 Corinthians 5:20.

God's best gifts – peace and salvation – are
not sought nor bought nor wrought.
They are free gifts of a gracious God.

'It is by grace you have been saved, through
faith – and this not from yourselves,
it is the gift of God – not by works,
so that no-one can boast.'
Ephesians 2:8, 9.

Peace and the unforced rhythms of grace.

'Are you tired? Worn out? Burned out on religion? Come to me. Get away with me and you'll recover your life. I'll show you how to take a real rest. Walk with me and work with me – watch how I do it. Learn the unforced rhythms of grace. I won't lay anything heavy or ill-fitting on you. Keep company with me and you'll learn to live freely and lightly.'
Matthew 11:28-30, MGE.

If a sense of injustice is robbing you of peace, remember a day is coming when all wrongs will be righted – and *everyone* will know!

'There is nothing concealed that will not be disclosed, or hidden that will not be made known.'
Matthew 10:26.

Peace is never assertive.

'The wisdom that comes from heaven is first of all pure. It is also peace loving, gentle at all times, and willing to yield to others.'
James 3:17, NLT.

The humble are those who are
secure – in Jesus.

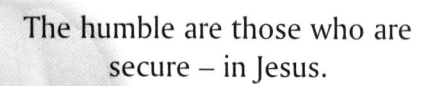

'Take my yoke upon you and learn from me,
for I am gentle and humble in spirit,
and you will find rest for your souls.'
Matthew 11:29.

The ability to forgive contributes to the
richness of life – and helps with
the peace aspect too.

'Smart people know how to hold their tongues;
their grandeur is to forgive and forget.'
Proverbs 19:11, MGE.

Repentance comes before forgiveness; and
forgiveness comes before peace.

'If my people, who are called by my name, will
humble themselves and pray and seek my face
and turn from their wicked ways, then will I
hear from heaven and will forgive their
sin and will heal their land.'
2 Chronicles 7:14.

God's presence is a place of peace
for the harrassed.

'God is a safe-house for the battered,
a sanctuary during bad times.
The moment you arrive, you relax;
you're never sorry you knocked.'
Psalm 9:9, MGE.

The real test of our peace is when our way traverses death valley.

'God, my shepherd!
I don't need a thing. You have bedded me down in lush meadows, you find me quiet pools to drink from.'
Psalm 23:1, 2, MGE.

Calvary was the price of our peace.

'He was wounded and crushed for our sins. He was beaten that we might have peace. He was whipped, and we were healed!'
Isaiah 53:5, NLT.

The best things in both time and eternity
are free. Free to you, that is: they
cost Christ Calvary.

'Hey there! All who are thirsty, come to the
water! Are you penniless?
Come anyway – buy and eat!
Come, buy your drinks, buy wine and milk.
Buy without money – everything's free.'
Isaiah 55:1, MGE.

Since you are what you eat, make sure your spiritual diet is of the best.

'Why do you spend your money on junk food, your hard-earned cash on cotton candy? Listen to me, listen well: Eat only the best, fill yourself with only the finest.'
Isaiah 55:2, MGE.

When you are down – God's strength comes into its own.

'To keep me from getting puffed up, I was given a thorn in my flesh. . . . Three different times I begged the Lord to take it away. Each time he said, "My gracious favour is all you need. My power works best in your weakness." '
2 Corinthians 12:7-9, NLT.

Of all the great questions of the day one is greater than all the rest: The Gospel of Christ.

'I am convinced that nothing can ever separate us from [God's] love. Death can't, and life can't. The angels can't, and the demons can't. Our fears for today, our worries about tomorrow, and even the powers of hell can't keep God's love away.'
Romans 8:38, NLT.

God does not love us because we are valuable.
We are valuable because God loves us.

'If I could speak in any language in heaven or
earth but didn't love others, I would only be
making meaningless noise.'
1 Corinthians 13:1, NLT.

Tap into peace power!

'The Christ you have to deal with is not a weak person outside you, but a tremendous power inside you.'
2 Corinthians 13:3, Phillips.

Jesus equals peace now and glory later.

'This is the secret: Christ lives in you,
and this is your assurance that
you will share in his glory.'
Colossians 1:27, NLT.

God's love is infinite in at
least three dimensions!

'I pray that you, being rooted and established in love, may have power, together with all the saints, to grasp how wide and long and high and deep is the love of Christ, and to know this love that surpasses knowledge.'
Ephesians 3:17-19.

How to be the ultimate high achiever.

'I can do everything through him
who gives me strength.'
Philippians 4:13.

Knowing Jesus is the secret of
contentment and peace.

'I have learned to be content whatever the
circumstances. I know what it is to be in need,
and I know what it is to have plenty.
I have learned the secret of being
content in any and every situation.'
Philippians 4:11, 12.

If you want peace, be careful on what
food you feed your mind.

'Whatever is true, whatever is noble, whatever
is right, whatever is pure, whatever is lovely,
whatever is admirable – if anything is excellent
or praiseworthy – think about such things.'
Philippians 4:8.

Jesus Christ is God's everything
for man's total need.

'I want you woven into a tapestry of love, in
touch with everything there is to know of God.
Then you will have minds confident and at rest,
focused on Christ, God's great mystery.'
Colossians 2:2, MGE.

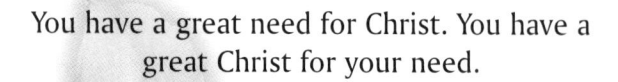

You have a great need for Christ. You have a great Christ for your need.

'I am sure that God, who began the good work within you, will continue his work until it is finally finished on that day when Christ Jesus comes back again.'
Philippians 1:6, NLT.

Cheer up! God's peace is yours!

'Finally, then, my brothers, cheer up! . . . accept
my encouragement . . . and live at peace.
So shall the God of love and peace
be ever with you.'
2 Corinthians 13:11, Phillips.

Peace follows pardon. Just ask!

'If we admit our sins – make a clean breast of them – he won't let us down; he'll be true to himself. He'll forgive our sins and purge us of all wrongdoing.'
1 John 1:9, MGE.

The God who handles the heavens
can handle your life.

'The heavens tell of the glory of God. The skies
display his marvellous craftsmanship. Day after
day they continue to speak; night after
night they make him known.'
Psalm 19: 1, 2, NLT.

The environment of peace.

'He who dwells in the shelter of the Most High
will rest in the shadow of the Almighty.'
Psalm 91:1.

New birth may occur in an instant, but the process of travelling from sinfulness to new life is a slow one.

' "I tell you the truth, no-one can see the kingdom of God unless he is born again. . . . You must be born again." '
John 3:3, 7.

Inner peace is based on assurance.

' "I tell you the truth, whoever hears my word and believes him who sent me *has* eternal life and will not be condemned; he has crossed over from death to life." '
John 5:24, italics supplied.

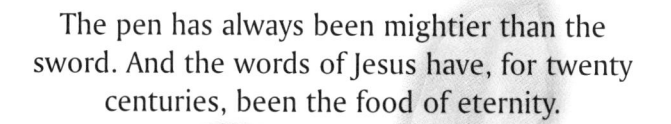

The pen has always been mightier than the sword. And the words of Jesus have, for twenty centuries, been the food of eternity.

'Simon Peter answered him, "Lord, to whom shall we go? You have the words of eternal life." '
John 6:68.

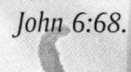

Ultimate, total security.

' "My sheep listen to my voice; I know them, and they follow me. I give them eternal life, and they will never perish; no-one can snatch them out of my hand. My Father, who has given them to me, is greater than all; no-one can snatch them out of my Father's hand." '
John 10:27-29.

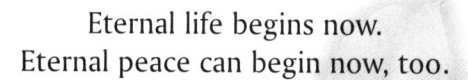

Eternal life begins now.
Eternal peace can begin now, too.

'I write these things to you who believe in the
name of the Son of God so that you may
know that you have eternal life.'
1 John 5:13.

God does have a plan!

' "You do not realise now what I am doing, but later you will understand." '
John 13:7.

The best – the *very* best – is yet to be.

' "Do not let your hearts be troubled. Trust in God; trust also in me. . . . If I go and prepare a place for you, I will come back and take you to be with me." '
John 14:1-3.

If what you're doing isn't working, have the flexibility to change it! Lifestyle changes may be indispensable to your peace.

'He takes us firmly by the hand and leads us into a radical life change.'
Romans 2:4, MGE.

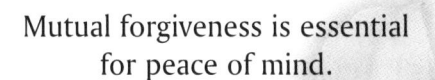

Mutual forgiveness is essential
for peace of mind.

'First forgive anyone you are holding a grudge
against, so that your Father in Heaven
will forgive your sins, too.'
Mark 11:25, NLT

Before you act ask, 'How will this course of action affect my life and my future?' Those who *don't* ask that question pay a high price.

'Let us lay aside every weight, . . .'
Hebrews 12:1, NKJV.

A trapeze artiste said, 'It takes repeated falls to convince you that the net will hold you; but once you know that, you forget about falling.'

'For though a righteous man falls seven times, he rises again.'
Proverbs 24:16.

Failure in your past can lead to fear in your future. Seek forgiveness and break the cycle of fear.

'With [God] on my side I'm fearless, afraid of no one and nothing.'
Psalm 27:1, MGE.

Life is too short to spend it as an inmate of the prison of your previous mistakes.

'You, my brothers, were called to be free.'
Galatians 5:13.

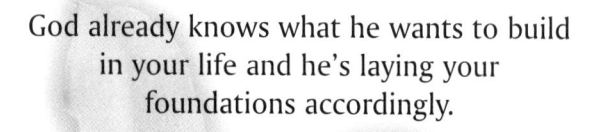

God already knows what he wants to build in your life and he's laying your foundations accordingly.

'Do not despise these small beginnings, for the Lord rejoices to see the work begin.'
Zechariah 4:10, NLT.

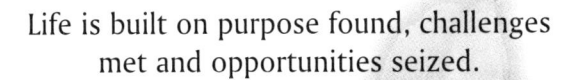

Life is built on purpose found, challenges met and opportunities seized.

'It's in Christ that we find out who we are and what we are living for.'
Ephesians 1:11, MGE.

Just as apology must precede reconciliation, so
repentance must precede pardon.
God is ready when you are!

'You are a forgiving God, gracious and
compassionate, slow to anger and
abounding in love.'
Nehemiah 9:17.

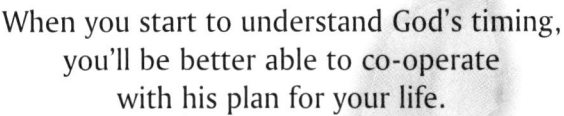

When you start to understand God's timing,
you'll be better able to co-operate
with his plan for your life.

'My times are in your hands.'
Psalm 31:15.

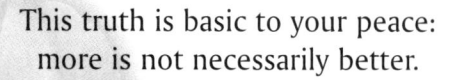

This truth is basic to your peace:
more is not necessarily better.

' "Watch out! Be on your guard against all kinds of greed; a man's life does not consist in the abundance of his possessions." '
Luke 12:15.

If you're worrying it means you've forgotten who's in charge.

' "I will trust and not be afraid.
The Lord, the Lord, is my strength and my song;
he has become my salvation." '
Isaiah 12:2.

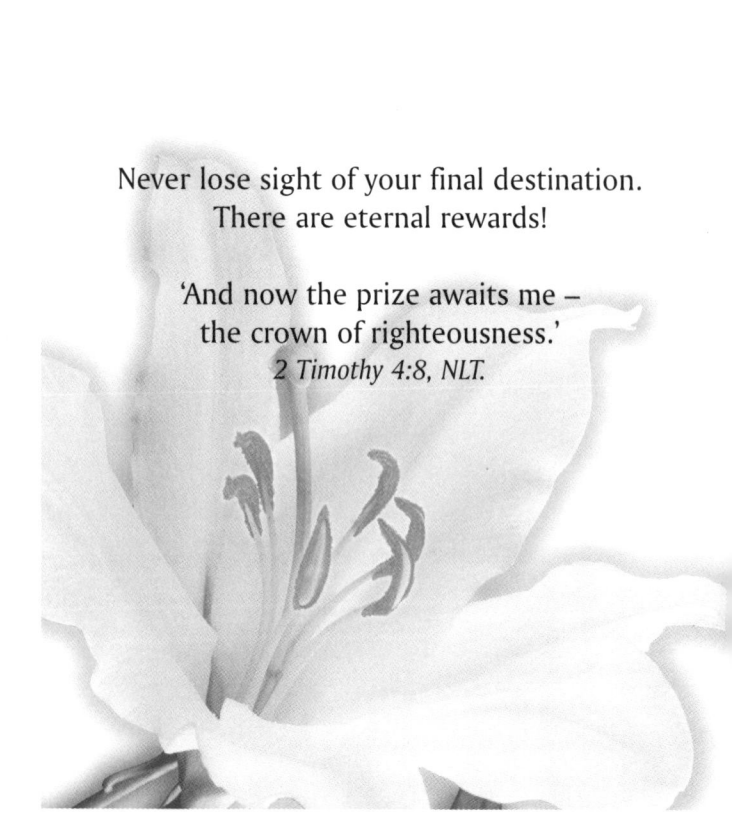

Never lose sight of your final destination.
There are eternal rewards!

'And now the prize awaits me –
the crown of righteousness.'
2 Timothy 4:8, NLT.

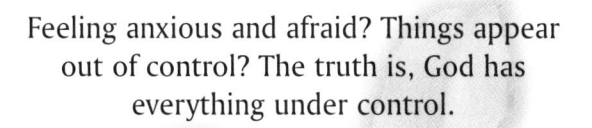

Feeling anxious and afraid? Things appear out of control? The truth is, God has everything under control.

' "Do not fear, for I am with you; do not be dismayed, for I am your God." '
Isaiah 41:10.

When things fall through or fizzle out, and people walk away, remember, God is holding the door open. . . .

'See, I have placed before you an open door that no-one can shut.'
Revelation 3:8.

Having a vision for your life will save you from three deadly enemies: indecision, indifference and impatience.

'Turn my eyes away from worthless things; preserve my life according to your word.'
Psalm 119:37.

Take the time to enjoy where you are, on the
way to where you are going.

'Enjoy your work . . . accept your lot in life.'
Ecclesiastes 5:19, Living Bible.

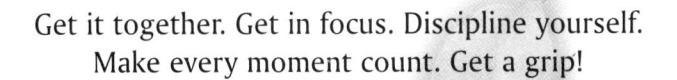

Get it together. Get in focus. Discipline yourself.
Make every moment count. Get a grip!

'Teach us to make the most of our time,
so that we may grow in wisdom.'
Psalm 90:12, NLT.

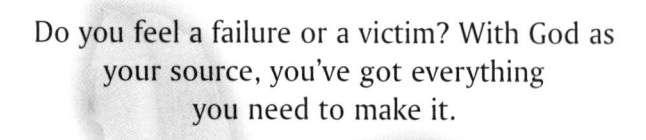

Do you feel a failure or a victim? With God as
your source, you've got everything
you need to make it.

'His divine power has given us
everything we need.'
2 Peter 1:3.

Going through a hard time? There are still things to thank God about. Identify what they are and get started.

'Praise be to the God . . . who comforts us in all our troubles.'
2 Corinthians 1:3, 4.

Your words are just photographs of your thoughts. The moment you express them, you empower them. Be 'blessing conscious' not 'burden conscious'.

'I groaned; I mused, and my spirit grew faint.'
Psalm 77:3.

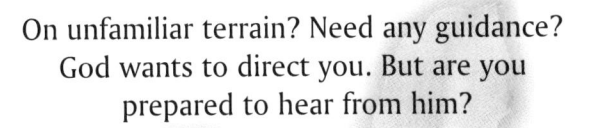

On unfamiliar terrain? Need any guidance?
God wants to direct you. But are you
prepared to hear from him?

'Along unfamiliar paths I will guide them.'
Isaiah 42:16.

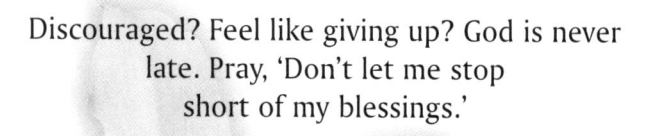

Discouraged? Feel like giving up? God is never late. Pray, 'Don't let me stop short of my blessings.'

'Do not throw away your confidence; it will be richly rewarded.'
Hebrews 10:35.

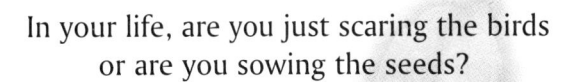

In your life, are you just scaring the birds or are you sowing the seeds?

'At the proper time, we will reap a harvest if we do not give up.'
Galatians 6:9.

Are you mired in your past?
Obsessing over your failures?

'I've blotted out your sins; they are gone. . . .
I have paid the price to set you free.' 'I am
bringing all my energies to bear on this
one thing: forgetting the past and
looking forward to what lies ahead.'
Isaiah 44:22; Philippians 3:13, Living Bible.

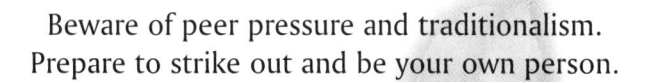

Beware of peer pressure and traditionalism.
Prepare to strike out and be your own person.

'Unlike the culture around you, always
dragging you down to its level. . . ,
God brings the best out of you.'
Romans 12:2, MGE.

With God there are no 'grey days'. When high hopes take a hike and dreams seem to be turning into nightmares, when good intentions get lost in a comedy of errors, it's time to count your blessings.

'Great is his faithfulness; his mercies begin afresh each day.'
Lamentations 3:23, NLT.

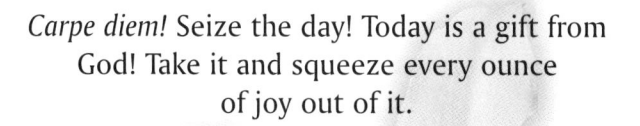

Carpe diem! Seize the day! Today is a gift from
God! Take it and squeeze every ounce
of joy out of it.

'This is the day the Lord has made;
let us rejoice and be glad in it.'
Psalm 118:24.

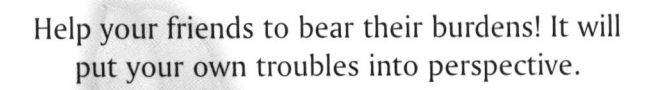

Help your friends to bear their burdens! It will put your own troubles into perspective.

'Share each other's troubles and problems, and in this way obey the law of Christ.'
Galatians 6:2, NLT.

Fear is an acrostic for False Evidence Appearing Real. Get God to handle fear and its causes.

'Be not afraid of sudden terror and panic. . . .'
Proverbs 3:25, Amplified Bible.

Grace is love that cares and stoops and rescues.

'Do you remember the generosity of
Jesus Christ? . . . . He was rich, yet he
became poor for your sakes so that
his poverty might make you rich.'
2 Corinthians 8:9, Phillips.

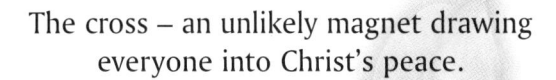

The cross – an unlikely magnet drawing everyone into Christ's peace.

' "When I am lifted up on the cross, I will draw everyone to myself." '
John 12:32, NLT.

The invitation of grace is 'Come!' And, when you come, the first gift you receive after forgiveness is peace.

'Whoever comes to me I will never drive away.'
John 6:37.

We are secure in the heart of God.

' "Can a mother forget the infant at her breast,
walk away from the baby she bore?
But even if mothers forget,
I'll never forget you – never.
Look, I've written your names on the backs of my hands." '
Isaiah 49:15, 16, MGE.

Bad religion destroys our peace.

'I am astonished that you are so quickly deserting the one who called you by the grace of Christ and are turning to a different gospel – which is really no gospel at all. Evidently some people are throwing you into confusion and are trying to pervert the gospel of Christ.'
Galatians 1:6, 7.

When we walk through the dark valley of meaninglessness and emptiness grace comes to relieve our pain and to bring us peace.

'Whoever is thirsty, let him come; and whoever wishes, let him take the free gift of the water of life.'
Revelation 22:17.

What is heavy about life is from ourselves; and what is light is the result of the grace of Christ and the love of God.

'Since we've compiled this long and sorry record as sinners . . . and proved that we are utterly incapable of living the glorious lives God wills for us, God did it for us. Out of sheer generosity he put us in rightstanding with himself. A pure gift. He got us out of the mess we're in and restored us to where he always wanted us to be. And he did it by means of Jesus Christ.'
Romans 3:22-24, MGE.

The gateway to peace.

'God sacrificed Jesus on the altar of the world to clear that world of sin. Having faith in him sets us in the clear. God decided on this course of action in full view of the public – to set the world in the clear with himself through the sacrifice of Jesus.'
Romans 3:25, 26, MGE.

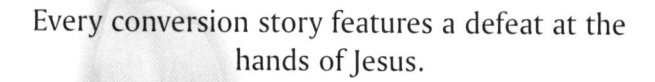

Every conversion story features a defeat at the hands of Jesus.

'God did not send his Son into the world to condemn the world, but to save the world through him.'
John 3:17.

Kindness recruits more for eternity than zeal, eloquence or learning ever did.

'Whoever drinks the water I give him will never thirst. Indeed, the water I give him will become in him a spring of water welling up to eternal life.'
John 4:14.

Jesus gives indestructible life, deathless life.

' "I am the resurrection and the life. He who believes in me will live, even though he dies; and whoever lives and believes in me will never die." '
John 11:25, 26.

God is a great leveller. No one need feel inferior, insecure or resentful with him. There are no 'important' and 'unimportant' people in God's eyes.

'Each of us will give an account of himself to God.'
Romans 14:12.